The Kims' Journey to Harmony

Barbara Vaille and
Jennifer QuinnWilliams

THE UNIVERSITY OF MICHIGAN PRESS

Ann Arbor

Copyright © by Barbara Vaille and Jennifer QuinnWilliams 2009
All rights reserved
Published in the United States of America
The University of Michigan Press
Manufactured in the United States of America
⊚ Printed on acid-free paper

2012   2011   2010   2009   4   3   2   1

ISBN-13: 978-0-472-03395-9

To the Reader:

This book was written for your pleasure. It is written in simple English for adult English language learners. We hope you will enjoy the story and learn English at the same time. When a character is speaking in Korean, the speech appears in *italics*. When a character is speaking in English, the type does not change. Hana's English is not always perfect, but it is written for authenticity of someone at her language level.

Happy Reading,
Barbara and Jennifer

Dedicated to Anita Bustamonte, our co-worker, who has piloted all our stories over the years.

CHAPTER
❖ 1 ❖

April

"Here you go, sir," the Korean Airlines flight attendant said. She passed a cup of orange juice to Hyo Kim. He was a clean-cut Korean man in his mid-thirties.

"Thank you."

"And here's your coffee, sir," she said. She set a cup down on the tray table in front of the large American man sitting next to Hyo.

"Thanks." Then, turning to Hyo, he said, "Are you going to the States for business?"

"No. My father died. I'm going to his funeral."

"Oh, I'm sorry to hear that. Was he visiting?"

"No. He was working with my older brother in their engineering company."

"Oh? Where?"

"In Denver, Colorado," said Hyo. He turned to look out the window. Clouds covered the Pacific Ocean, but the sun was shining brightly. It was raining in Seoul, Korea, when he waved goodbye to his wife and two children three hours earlier. He wondered if the sun would be shining in Denver.

1

"Your English is quite good," the American said. "Have you been to the U.S. before?"

"Yes, I studied at the University of Iowa," answered Hyo.

"What was your major?"

"Civil engineering."

Hyo looked out the window again. The man next to him was like many Americans he remembered, friendly and curious. It reminded Hyo of when he was in Iowa at the university 12 years earlier. He enjoyed his time in the United States, and he felt comfortable with Americans. He was curious about this man and why he was in Korea.

"Why were you in Korea, sir?" Hyo asked.

"For business. I work for an import/export company. We're working with a new client and my boss wanted me to meet the management team. We like to get to know who we're working with. It's good for business. By the way, my name's John Baker," he said. He held out his hand to Hyo. They shook hands.

"Hyo Kim. Nice to meet you," replied Hyo.

The two men talked for almost an hour about business and engineering in Korea and the U.S. Then the flight attendant served them lunch. After eating, they continued their conversation. They told each other about their families. John was from Austin, Texas. He was a widower.

"My wife died six years ago. I miss her. We were married for 35 years. I'm lucky, though, because my two daughters and their families live in Austin. I have five grandchildren. They keep me running! And I get along real well with my sons-in-law. I got one of them a job in the same company where I work. Here, let me show you some pictures."

Hyo looked at the smiling people with straight white teeth.

"This was from last summer at our Fourth of July barbeque. These people are my neighbors, but there's one granddaughter and here's another." He continued pointing out his family to Hyo, who politely looked and listened. "Do you have any pictures of your family?" John asked Hyo.

"Just one." He reached for his wallet and took out a picture of himself with his family. "This is my wife, Hana, my son, Dak Ho, and my daughter, Cho Hee. He is ten years old. She is six."

"Nice looking family you have there," said John.

"Thank you," said Hyo.

"Don't you want to move to the States and be near your mother and brother?"

"No. My wife and I are happy living in Korea. She is established in her work. She's an artist, and she teaches pottery at the university in Seoul. The children go to one of the best schools in the city."

The 12-hour flight to Los Angeles was smooth but long and tiring. The men got up a few times to stretch their legs. They also read the newspaper and magazines and worked on their laptops. After six hours of flying, the pilot announced that they

3

had crossed the International Date Line, and it was now the day before. People adjusted their watches. The sun was going down. Hyo tried to sleep, but his mind was full of thoughts of his father. Shortly before landing in Los Angeles the two men continued their conversation.

"Did your kids know your father?" John asked Hyo.

"My son remembers him. We live in my parents' house in Seoul. They moved to Denver seven years ago to live with my brother and his family. My parents came back to Korea once to visit. My daughter only knew him from that visit."

"Too bad your wife and kids couldn't come with you."

"Yes. But it is very expensive."

"Well, I've enjoyed talking with you. Best of luck to you and your family. Here, let me give you my business card. It has my email address on it in case you need it. You never know," said John. He passed the card to Hyo.

"Thank you. And here is my card if you are ever back in Seoul," said Hyo.

It was almost 3:00 in the morning, but the lights of the city of Los Angeles lit up the night sky. The plane made its descent into the LAX airport, landed, and taxied to the gate.

The passengers walked down the jetway and into the terminal toward Baggage Claim and Customs. The long lines moved quickly. When it was

Hyo's turn, he gave the agent his passport and answered some questions about why he was in the United States. The agent stamped his passport.

Hyo got some breakfast at a coffee shop on the concourse and then went to the gate to wait for his flight to Denver.

The plane was half empty. Hyo had enjoyed talking to John, but he was relieved that no one sat next to him on this flight. He was very tired. In the past week he learned about his father's death, made plans to take time off from work, and left his family. He needed some rest. Hyo slept.

The flight attendant's voice woke him up. "We are now making our descent into Denver International Airport."

Hyo got his suitcase from the baggage claim carousel. Then he called his brother, Kwan, on his cell phone. Kwan told Hyo to wait outside the doors for arriving passengers.

"I'll pick you up there," he said.

Soon they were on the big interstate highway, I-70, heading into the city.

"Kwan, how are you? Is Mother well? How is your family?" Hyo asked.

"We are fine, sad, but fine. I'm glad you arrived safely. Mother will be happy to see you."

The two brothers had only seen each other once since Kwan and his family moved to Colorado seven years ago. They talked by phone and emailed every month. They knew the events that happened in each

5

others' lives, but not the deeper feelings that could be detected by noticing subtle looks and gestures.

Hyo glanced at Kwan. He was still the older brother that Hyo looked up to when they were younger, but he had changed. Kwan was more serious and worried looking. His face was white from lack of sleep. He had gained weight that seemed to give him stooped shoulders.

"*Tell me about Father,*" said Hyo. "*I know he was slowing down and couldn't work as much as he did a few years ago.*"

"*Yes, that's true. And it bothered him. He didn't feel that he was contributing enough to the family or to the company. He felt like he was disappointing everyone. It was hard to watch. You remember how he was. We used to call him The Commander because he was always in charge.*"

"I remember," Hyo said. "*It was like that before he moved here with you. He didn't like retirement very much. He didn't have enough to do. That made it hard for me. In his eyes, I never did anything well enough. I felt I had to bow to his wishes and do what he wanted me to do, not what I wanted.*"

"I understand," said Kwan.

"*And you know how hard his retirement was for Mother. She took out her frustrations on Hana. It was a good decision for us when they decided to come here to live.*"

Kwan sighed. His shoulders sagged a little more.

"Please, let's not talk about this now. There is still a lot to do before the funeral the day after tomorrow.

Hyo realized his mistake of talking about his negative thoughts to his brother. It was not the time or the place.

"I'm sorry. You're right. Tell me what needs to be done. I want to help."

Kwan's house was near the Flower Park on Speer Boulevard. It was a small, red brick house on a pleasant street lined with tall shade trees. Mi Sun, Kwan's wife, had planted many spring bulbs, now in bloom, that decorated both sides of the path leading up to the front porch. The door opened. The brothers' mother stepped out, followed by Mi Sun.

Hyo went to his mother and hugged her. Then, with a slight bow of his head, he said, *"Mother, how are you feeling? Are you in good health?"*

"I'm fine, my son," she said. *"Come in."*

Inside, Mi Sun called to her daughter, *"Su Jin, come and greet your uncle."* The 16-year-old girl looked up from the computer and smiled at Hyo.

As the oldest male, Kwan was in charge of all the funeral preparations. He had already invited friends and acquaintances to the funeral. Here in the United States, only some of the traditional Korean customs were followed.

Fortunately, the family had been at Hyo and Kwan's father's bedside when he died. They had all cried and continued to cry when people came by to

7

pay their respects. Hyo knew that his mother was disappointed that he had not arrived before his father died, and he was sorry, too. His father's decline in health was unexpected. His death came quickly.

The funeral was in the chapel at the cemetery. A large picture of their father and bouquets of white chrysanthemums were near the casket. All the family wore white armbands with a black stripe in the center. After the service, there was a reception. Hyo and Kwan stood beside their mother as the mourners came in to express their sympathies. Their father would be cremated, so there was no burial ceremony.

Hyo stayed in Denver for a week after the funeral. Much of the family conversation was about his father. They told stories about growing up in Korea. Su Jin heard many of these for the first time. They laughed and cried.

Kwan took Hyo to his engineering company. He was the owner and president now that their father was dead. It was a small firm of 50 employees. They designed and constructed roads and highways. Kwan explained that they were trying to meet a deadline to finish one project and were making the preliminary designs for another.

Hyo observed quietly. The offices were clean and bright. There was a hum of activity as the engineers talked to each other about the blueprints of the projects. Hyo noticed several women, but most were men. He felt Kwan's eyes on him.

"You have done well, Kwan. This is a good company."

"It is only luck, and our father's hard work," Kwan answered, protesting politely. *"Father had great hopes for the business. You know he always wanted the three of us to work together."*

Hyo looked at his brother in disbelief. This wasn't true. His father never said anything at all to him about that.

Kwan continued, *"He left you money, Hyo. He wanted you to move to Denver with your family and work here in the company. Now I do, too. We need your help."*

CHAPTER
❖ 2 ❖

June

Hana looked around her. These basement rooms were her new home in the United States. She tried not to show her disappointment. The carpet was gray, the walls were gray, and there were only three small windows in the living room for the sun to shine through. Her house in Korea was much larger. There, she was lucky. After Hyo's parents moved to the USA seven years ago, she and Hyo and the children had lived in his parents' house. Most of her friends lived in apartments in large high-rise buildings. But this basement apartment was not nearly as nice as the apartments of her friends in Korea.

She turned to her sister-in-law, Mi Sun. *"Thank you for your hospitality. We will be very comfortable here."*

Mi Sun smiled and waved her hands at the walls. *"The last tenant painted this all gray. We can paint it a different color to make it more cheerful."*

Hana wasn't sure how to answer. She didn't know there was a tenant before. Maybe she and Hyo were depriving Mi Sun and her family of income.

Even stranger, it seemed like Mi Sun was saying that Hana and Mi Sun could paint the small apartment themselves. Was Hana now a laborer? Was living here going to be as bad as when she lived with Hyo's parents in their house?

She didn't show her thoughts. Instead she said, *"Oh, yes."*

Mi Sun was perceptive. She noticed Hana's hesitation. She said, *"Americans like to have projects. They work on their own homes all the time. They think it's fun to paint, remodel, and fix things by themselves, without help. I like it, too."*

Hana was grateful for the explanation and grateful that her sister-in-law seemed to understand her. *"I never painted a wall, but maybe I would enjoy it,"* she said.

Mi Sun showed Hana the tiny bathroom and the two small bedrooms of the basement apartment. Then she took her into a dark, narrow kitchen.

"Don't worry, we'll eat meals together upstairs," she said. *"But you can make tea and snacks for the kids down here whenever you like."*

Hana nodded. She tried not to show her gloom. She missed Korea already, after only a few hours in the USA. Where would she do her pottery? How would she have any privacy in this cramped house, with all Hyo's family? She followed Mi Sun up the stairs to the sunny kitchen on the first floor. There, her two children, Dak Ho and Cho Hee, were sitting

11

quietly at the kitchen table. Their grandmother was asking questions about school and hobbies. They answered politely, but Hana could tell they felt very shy with the older woman.

Kwan and Hyo were on the back deck. They were talking seriously with each other. Mother-in-Law glanced at Hana. *"My sons are having a talk. Take them some drinks. Maybe they would like something to eat."*

Hana looked at Mi Sun in dismay. This wasn't her house. She didn't even know where the glasses were. Mi Sun gave her a little smile.

"What a good idea, Mother-in-Law," she said. *"I have some soft drinks and Kwan loves American pretzels. So salty. Hana, the glasses are there,"* she pointed to a cupboard.

Hana got the glasses out. Mi Sun stood beside her and poured pretzels into a bowl. *"Thank goodness you are here, little sister,"* she whispered. *"Now, we can follow the old lady's orders together!"* She winked at Hana. Hana grinned in surprise. Maybe life under the same roof as Mi Sun wouldn't be so bad after all.

That night, after the kids were in bed, Hana and Hyo sat in their gray living room, watching a small color TV.

"Hana, did we make a mistake?" asked Hyo. *"When Kwan told me that Father wanted me to work in the business, I felt like I had to say yes. But now*

12

that we're here, I already feel like I'm being smothered."

"No, we did the right thing," said Hana. She tried to sound very confident, but she didn't feel very confident. "We are a family. Your brother needed you. And I really like Mi Sun! I didn't remember that she is so funny and friendly."

Hyo sighed. "Well, Mother is the same as before. Ordering you around."

"Yes. But Hyo, that's her way. She's very traditional. I will just try to make her happy."

Hyo put his arm around her. Hana put her head on his shoulder. They sat and stared at the television for a while.

"I forgot to tell you," said Hana. "Mi Sun told me there's an English class in the school where the kids will go. They have a summer program. I can start on Monday."

"That's good," murmured Hyo. He sounded like he was about to fall asleep.

"And she told me about a place where I can go to see about making pottery."

"Mmm-hmm. One thing at a time," said Hyo, with a yawn.

In the morning, even though it was Saturday, Hyo and Kwan went to the office.

"We'll just work for two or three hours," said Kwan. "I'll tell you about the projects and you can arrange your office."

13

Mi Sun said to Hana, *"Do you want to go shopping? I'll show you where the big Korean market is and we can go to a clothing store I like."*

"That would be nice, but what about Dak Ho and Cho Hee? They probably won't want to go to a clothing store."

Mother-in-Law spoke up. *"Take all of us to the Korean market. Then, bring Dak Ho, Cho Hee, and me home. We'll spend some time getting to know each other."*

Dak Ho and Cho Hee looked at their mother with dismay. They didn't want to be left with their grandmother.

Mi Sun looked surprised. *"Mother-in-Law, you don't usually go to the market. It's a long way from here. You just tell me what to buy. Why do you want to go today?"*

"Now that Hana is here, she can do the shopping and cooking," said Mother-in-Law. *"You and Kwan work hard, and Hyo will also be very busy. It's time for Hana to take on some responsibility for the family. I'll show her what I like, and then I won't have to go with her again."*

Mi Sun said, *"Of course, Mother-in-Law, what a good idea. But you don't like to shop. I know what kinds of food you like, and I will be happy to show Hana. Also, I was planning to shop at the clothing store first, then go to the Korean market. It's a warm day and I don't want to leave the food in the car."*

Hana stayed silent. She admired the easy way

Mi Sun talked to Mother-in-Law, with just the right amount of affection and respect. She was afraid if she spoke, her words might sound childish and unhappy.

Mother-in-Law thought for a minute. *"I'm not sure you know all the ingredients I like for making kimchi. I want to show Hana how to make it."*

"Make kimchi?" Hana asked. *"I've never made it. My mother never made it either! Mother-in-Law, I remember you bought it in Korea, too."*

"The kimchi in the store here is no good," said Mother-in-Law. *"When I was a young wife, all the women made kimchi together. You can make it for us after I teach you how."*

Almost all Korean meals included kimchi, a spicy fermented vegetable dish. But in Korea there were many excellent places to buy high-quality kimchi. Hana never expected she would have to make it. She decided this would be a good way to develop a relationship with Mother-in-Law like Mi Sun had.

"I would be very happy to learn from you, Mother-in-Law," she said. *"And if you want to personally show me the ingredients I would be grateful."*

Hana's children looked relieved. They didn't have to stay home with grandmother.

But Mother-in-Law now changed her mind. *"No, Mi Sun is right. You two go, and I'll stay home with the children."*

15

"Su Jin will stay home, too," said Mi Sun. *"Go and find her,"* she said to the children. *"Ask her to take you to the park."*

Mi Sun and Hana got their purses and left. As they drove out of Mi Sun's neighborhood, Hana noticed that the roads became wider. Instead of older brick houses with tidy yards, there were businesses and apartment buildings. They were driving from the urban neighborhood where Mi Sun and Kwan lived to the suburbs, where the Korean grocery store was.

"Why did you choose to live in the older part of town?" Hana asked Mi Sun.

"Mostly because it's close to the building Father-in-Law chose for the office," said Mi Sun. *"And Kwan likes the older houses. I like the neighborhood."*

The two women talked about what living in Denver was like, compared to Korea. Again, Hana was glad that Mi Sun was here to help her. They talked about getting a driver's license for Hana and what kinds of activities they could find for the kids to do over the summer. When they got to the clothing store, they continued to talk and laugh as they looked at summer clothes and sandals. Then, they went on to the Korean market where Mi Sun showed Hana what foods Mother-in-Law preferred.

"I don't really like to cook," Hana confessed to Mi Sun. *"I hope I can satisfy Mother-in-Law."*

"Don't worry. I love to cook! I'm not going to stop

cooking just because Mother-in-Law thinks it should be your responsibility. We'll cook together. It will be fun. You know, Mother-in-Law just wants life to be smooth and easy for her sons. Once she sees that you and Hyo are good parents and have a good marriage, she'll probably stop being so bossy."

"Do you think so?" asked Hana. "Is she still bossy with you?"

Mi Sun smiled. *"Well, yes she is!"*

"There's not much hope for me then, is there?" laughed Hana. But, there, having fun with Mi Sun, it did seem like things might be okay.

Later that day, she didn't feel so optimistic. As soon as they got home, Mother-in-Law wanted to start the kimchi. Hana was tired. She felt dizzy and had a slight headache. This was her first day in Denver. She was jet-lagged and not used to Denver's high altitude. Everything she read in Korea before she came to Denver said she should get plenty of rest for the first few days and drink a lot of water.

She said, *"If I could just sleep for half an hour, I think I could help with the kimchi. But I feel like I can't even keep my eyes open right now."*

Mother-in-Law started to protest, but Mi Sun soothed her. *"Mother-in-Law, let's have a cup of tea and watch a bit of that Korean movie you like. Then, when Hana wakes up, we'll all make kimchi together, just like you did when you were a young woman."*

17

Mother-in-Law smiled at Mi Sun. *"Oh, yes. We women all worked hard on that kimchi when I was young, but we enjoyed being together. And that was the best kimchi in the neighborhood. Everyone wanted a taste."*

After Hana's nap Mother-in-Law was no longer in a good mood. She was remembering the happy days when she was a young woman in Korea. Everything Hana did was wrong.

"You don't really hold the knife right," complained Mother-in-Law. *"And, if you don't speed it up a little, we'll be here until midnight."*

Later, Mother-in-Law said that she had put too much salt in the water the cabbage soaked in. After that, she said there was not enough chili powder in the spice mixture. Then, when they were mixing the kimchi in a big bowl, she said Hana was not gentle enough and was bruising the cabbage so that it let off a bad smell.

Hana tried to remain patient and kind. She didn't say that she knew how to be gentle. She was a potter and had to be very careful with the vases and bowls she made. She thanked Mother-in-Law for showing her how to make the kimchi and offered to make her a cup of tea after all the hard work.

"No, I want a nice glass of water. Then we'll make dinner for the men. I'll teach you how to make Hyo's favorite dish."

Hana felt like a new bride. After ten years of marriage, she knew what Hyo's favorite dish was.

18

She thought she probably knew more about him now than his mother did. Hyo and Kwan were still not home, and it was getting late in the afternoon. Was this how every day with her mother-in-law going to be?

CHAPTER
❖ 3 ❖

July

Hyo sat in his office thinking about changes he wanted to suggest to two small road projects. They were small, inexpensive changes that would make the roads more beautiful for people driving on them. In Korea, Hyo's company had a reputation for building beautiful, functional structures. Here, Kwan's company had a reputation for saving money on projects.

Hyo talked to Kwan about his ideas that afternoon. Kwan said, *"Don't tell me about your arty ideas. Father spent several months working on this. I checked the plans over myself. They work and we're under budget. We're not changing them now."*

In Korea, the younger brother obeyed the wishes and orders of the older brother. But for the last seven years in Korea, Hyo was independent. He was his own boss. Now, he was having a hard time fitting back into the traditional Korean role of the younger brother. He wanted to work with his brother as an equal. He wanted both of them to be respectful of each other's ideas. This was not how things were. All the projects were already in progress, and there seemed to be no way for Hyo to contribute his expertise. Why did he and his family move here from Korea if there was no real contribution he could make to the company?

Kwan was out in the field. Hyo had nothing else to do, so he took out the plans for the major highway project that Kwan was managing. Their company was selected to build the bridges over the highway for all of the major streets. Kwan had said to Hyo, *"Don't waste your time looking at those plans. Supervise the other project. Father and I already went over those plans several times."*

However, Hyo liked to practice converting figures from Centigrade to Fahrenheit. In Korea, all work was done in the metric system. He knew the American Customary System of miles, inches, and Fahrenheit because he had attended an American university, but he liked to practice the conversions to meters, centimeters, and Centigrade. He wanted to be good at using both.

Soon he was imagining the new highway and bridges. Denver really needed this renovation. The traffic at the south end of the city was stretching the limits of the present road system.

Hyo looked at the calculations for the bridges' expansion joints. The expansion joints were special connections between parts of the bridge. If the weather was cold, the joints allowed the bridge to expand. If the weather was hot, the joints allowed the bridge to contract. This kept the bridge from

21

being damaged by the weather. The calculations seemed fine at first. Hyo entered the data into the formulas on his computer. Something was wrong. His results didn't match his father's. He tried again, with the same results. And again. Same thing.

What could be the reason? They both used the same formulas. Hyo thought about his father. His whole career was in Korea. It was not until after he retired that he moved to the United States to help Kwan. Of course the American Customary System was awkward for him, since he had never used it before.

Hyo was beginning to think in American Customary and work problems out without converting them into metric and back again. Suddenly Hyo had an insight: It was like learning another language. At first, language learners like to translate. But only when a learner can think in the new language does he or she become "fluent," or able to speak easily and naturally.

Did his father ever become fluent in the American Customary System, or was he still translating? Hyo tried thinking like his father. He took all the numbers and changed them to metric. Then he put those numbers into the formulas on his computer. Then he converted them back to American Customary. Yes, there. Hyo found the mathematical error.

The difference was small, but could be very bad for the company. His father suggested using one kind of expansion joint, but Hyo's calculations showed that another type of joint should be used. Somehow he needed to tell Kwan, but Kwan was still out in the field.

Hyo glanced at the clock on the wall. 11:50. Time for lunch. He didn't feel very hungry. What he really wanted to do was go to his neighborhood studio back in Korea and spend an hour doing taekwondo. In Korea, a studio was two blocks away from his office. Here in Denver, in Capitol Hill, he had not found one at all. He walked to work instead of driving most days. But that exercise wasn't enough for him. He knew he was getting out of shape and losing muscle tone. He walked home for lunch.

"What's the matter, Hyo? asked Hana when he came in the apartment. *"You look worried."*

"It's nothing. Just a problem at work, but I'll figure it out."

"Tell me about it."

Hyo took a deep breath. *"I'm trying to understand where I fit in. But when I talk to Kwan, he says no to every idea. He and Father were much better partners. I don't enjoy this kind of engineering. I liked what I did in Korea because I could be creative. But here there's no place for creativity. The worst part is that I can't talk to Kwan about it. He won't listen."*

Hana said, *"I remember that even in Korea, you and Kwan sometimes had trouble talking without offending each other."*

"It's true. And to make things worse, this after-noon I was practicing converting Fahrenheit and Centigrade on the plans for the main project. I found some miscalculations that Father made which could make the bridges unsafe. Kwan's out in the field, but I'm afraid he will be angry with me again for looking at the plans at all. I guess I'll wait a few days and think about how to tell him."

The next day, Hana held the classroom door open for Sony, another student from Korea.

"Karen is such a good teacher. I like writing in my journal. Her responses are helping me write better. And I really like the topics when we practice speaking. Today's lesson was interesting. I enjoyed learning about recycling in the USA," said Hana.

"It was okay. But we live in an apartment, and they don't have recycling there, so it wasn't very useful for me."

"That's too bad. The city comes every other week and picks up the paper and other recyclables from the purple containers."

"Lucky for you," said Sony.

Hana was quiet. Lucky? She didn't feel lucky. There was still tension between her and her mother-in-law. But most of all, she was worried about Hyo.

24

"*Hana?*" Sony's voice startled her. "*Are you okay?*"

"*Oh, sorry. I was just thinking of something,*" said Hana.

"*Today my baby's staying with a friend from church. Do you want to go get some lunch?*" asked Sony.

Hana hesitated. "*I don't know. My mother-in-law talked about cooking this afternoon. . . .*"

"*Maybe you can call her and do it later. What about your kids?*"

"*They're in day camp all day, so that's alright. And my sister-in-law is at work.*"

"*Great,*" said Sony. "*Where shall we go? There's a little restaurant near my apartment building. Do you want to go there?*"

"*Sure,*" said Hana.

Sony drove east past Colorado Boulevard.

"*We're near the big Korean grocery store, aren't we?*" asked Hana.

"*Yes. It's a few blocks south of here on Parker Road.*"

"*You live far from class,*" said Hana. "*How long does it take for you to drive to school?*"

"*About 20 minutes in good weather. That's my apartment building over there,*" said Sony, pointing at a blonde brick building. There were several buildings just alike surrounded by pine trees. "*And here's the restaurant,*" she said.

At lunch, the two women talked about their backgrounds and families. Sony was a pharmacist in Korea. *"I imagined I would love staying home with my baby all day while we're here in the U.S. But I miss adult conversation. I'm so glad I found the English class. I thought about trying to get a job. Unfortunately, I don't have the right visa to work here, and my English isn't good enough yet."*

"What does your husband do?" asked Hana.

"He's doing research at National Jewish Hospital. In two years, we'll return to Korea."

"Do you take him to work?"

"No. He takes two buses to get to work so I can have the car, but we like the apartment complex, so we don't mind. There are several international families living here. One of my neighbors is from Morocco. The family across the hall is from Turkey. Sometimes the cooking smells are strange, but it's interesting," Sony said, laughing.

Sony drove Hana home.

"See you tomorrow in class. Thanks. This was fun," said Hana.

It was quiet inside the house. Her mother-in-law's door was closed. Hana breathed a sigh of relief. She wanted to have some time to herself before everyone came home.

Hana went downstairs. The windows of the apartment were shaded by the bushes in the side yard. The gray walls were gloomy. She turned on the light, but the room was still dark. Maybe a more

26

cheerful color of paint would make her and Hyo feel better. She heard the back door open. Hana went upstairs to see who it was. Mi Sun greeted her.

"Hi, Hana."

"Hi, Mi Sun. You're home early. Didn't you have to work this afternoon?"

"I finished everything so my boss said I could leave."

"I just got home, too. Do you have any plans this afternoon?"

"No. Why?" asked Mi Sun.

"Do you remember when you suggested that we paint the walls downstairs? We've all been so busy since we got here that we haven't thought about it. But now that we're more settled, I suddenly noticed how dark they are. Do you really think we could paint them ourselves?"

"We won't know until we try! Let's go to the home improvement store and see what we need."

The door of their mother-in-law's room opened. She marched up to Hana and Mi Sun.

"Did you sleep well?" asked Mi Sun.

"How could I sleep with you two talking? And what's this about painting downstairs? Don't you think you should have asked me? Hana, I blame you. Before you came, Mi Sun asked my opinion about everything."

Hana was silent. Mi Sun said, *"Mother-in-Law, would you like to come with us to shop for paint?"*

27

"*Who will be here when the children come home? Did you think of that?*"

Hana said, "*You are right. I'll stay. It was a silly idea to paint.*"

Mother-in-Law spoke. "*I don't agree. Hyo is too quiet. He never makes jokes like he used to. We were always laughing. Maybe if the walls were a brighter color, like yellow, Hyo would be his old self again. You two go. It is too crowded at that store for me.*"

Mi Sun and Hana had fun choosing the paint. There were so many different colors and hues. They finally decided on a light yellow for the living room. Then they found a "how-to" book on painting. It told them the other supplies they needed.

They both put tape around the windows and lay plastic drop cloths on the floor. Mi Sun painted the walls with the roller. Hana painted the trim around the windows and doors with a brush. Then they switched. Hana was slow at first, but she got better quickly.

They were cleaning up at six, when Kwan and Hyo came home together. They inspected their wives' work.

"*This looks great. What a difference!*" said Hyo.

"*Good. What's for dinner?*" said Kwan. The other three looked at him.

Mi Sun said quickly, "*We have some ground beef. Let's make hamburgers on the grill. We'll season them Korean-style. Plain American hamburgers are too bland.*"

28

The two women went up to the kitchen to prepare the hamburgers, make a salad, and get the condiments for the burgers. They worked easily together. When everything was ready, they took it outside.

"Kwan, you like to grill meat. Do you want to grill the hamburgers?" asked Mi Sun.

"I'm tired. Hyo can do it. He doesn't have enough to do," said Kwan.

Mi Sun laughed, but no one else was laughing. She looked around at the adults. Everyone was stunned into silence. Hyo found his voice first.

"Of course, I'll be happy to grill. Where is the spatula?"

Soon the smell of the burgers made Hana realize how hungry she was after painting.

"Cho Hee," she called to her daughter. *"Set the table. And Su Jin, pour the water, please."*

Everyone sat around the picnic table on the deck in the backyard. The children chattered about their day. Su Jin asked them questions. She enjoyed having her cousins living with them. It gave her a taste of what it was like to have siblings.

The adults ate quietly. After dinner, Kwan went in to watch TV. The kids went to the park to play ball. Hyo helped the women clear the table.

"Hyo, this is not your job. Hana can do it," said his mother.

"It's fine, Mother. I don't mind helping at all."

"No, I insist."

29

Hyo put down the plates he was carrying and went downstairs.

In the kitchen, Hana's mother-in-law turned to her and said, *"What has happened to you? Where is your respect for my sons? Is it because you are taking those English classes? Are they making you forget your duty as a good Korean wife? As long as you are living here, he will not be treated as a servant. He and Kwan work hard for us. Now that their father has died, Kwan is the head of this family. He knows what is best for us, and he is helping Hyo and you as well. Your job is to take care of their needs at home. Watch out! You are being selfish. Think of your children. What kind of role model are you for them?"*

Hana listened to her mother-in-law's tirade. Her eyes were cast down respectfully. She was glad no one could see the tears welling up in them.

"Of course, Mother-in-Law. You are right. Please forgive me."

Hana turned to go. She passed Mi Sun, whose face was filled with compassion, and went downstairs to the apartment.

Twice in one day. Could things get much worse?

CHAPTER
❖ 4 ❖

August

Every morning Hana looked out the kitchen window. She saw the Rocky Mountains. They loomed majestically in the west, inviting the Kim family to come for a visit, but Hana and Hyo hadn't left Denver since they arrived there. So, on the weekend, they decided to take the kids and drive to the mountains. Hyo looked up Rocky Mountain National Park on the Internet and printed a map.

Hana told Mi Sun they were going for a hike. She hoped that Mi Sun and Mother-in-Law would not want to go. Kwan was already at the office. Mi Sun said she was busy and, as usual, Mother-in-Law was against Hana's plans.

"Why are you going so far? You could just go to the park. Kwan needs Hyo in the office. Remember, 'A mountain is built one speck of dust at a time'."

Hyo and Hana were surprised. Mother-in-Law was using the Korean proverb to say that goals could only be reached by a lot of hard work. But Hyo felt like his time at the office was wasted, since Kwan wouldn't let him do very much. And Hana felt

31

like Hyo was always at work. He spent very little time with her.

Hyo said, *"Look, I've planned the whole trip very well. It will take two-and-a-half hours to reach Rocky Mountain National Park. We'll enjoy the scenery on the drive, take a short hike, have a picnic, and be back by dinner time. Kwan doesn't need me today."*

As usual Mi Sun was the peacemaker. *"Remember when you and Father-in-Law came to Denver? We used to go skiing sometimes, and you two would come up with us and sit in the lodge and play with Su Jin. It was fun."*

Mother-in-Law smiled a little. *"Yes. I remember."* She glared at Hana. *"But I'm not going to come with you to take care of the children."*

"Oh, no! We want to take them. And Su Jin if she wants to come. Today you'll be free to enjoy yourself."

Even though Mother-in-Law only took care of the children once in a while, this seemed to make her happy.

Su Jin wanted to come, so the five of them started off. They decided to stop at the Korean grocery store first to get some picnic things. Hana and the children went into the grocery store, and Hyo walked next door to a taekwondo studio he noticed. He watched a group of students in crisp white uniforms as they practiced a form. They all moved through the form's paces at the same time. Then an instructor came out and gave them some directions

32

and they started over. How Hyo missed the discipline and beauty of his daily taekwondo practice. In Korea, he worked hard for years to become a fifth-degree black belt, a master. Here, he didn't have a place to work out.

A tall, muscular blonde man with clear brown eyes came out of the door of the studio. "Are you interested in taekwondo?" he asked.

"Yes! I used to practice in Korea," Hyo answered.

The man started speaking in fluent Korean. *"Oh, I studied with some great masters in Korea. I lived there for 10 years."*

It was good to hear an American speaking his language. He and the man, Tom, talked about taekwondo and the studio for the next 10 minutes. Tom told Hyo to come back and try working out there. *"The first five sessions are free,"* he said.

Hana and the children came out of the grocery store. Hyo thanked Tom and joined them at the car.

"I was talking to Tom, the owner of that taekwondo studio," he told Hana. *"He offered me five free sessions. I'm going to try it after work on Monday."*

Hana knew how much Hyo missed taekwondo. He felt as passionate about it as she felt about pottery. *"Good idea,"* she said. *"Maybe you won't feel so bored and frustrated at work if you have taekwondo to look forward to at the end of the day."*

Suddenly she remembered that Kwan's daugh-

33

ter, Su Jin, was sitting in the back seat of the car. She hoped Su Jin didn't say anything to her father about Hyo's unhappiness with his job. To stop Hyo from saying any more, she turned to the kids.

"Okay, now we have a beautiful drive coming up. I've heard there are buffalo, goats, and sometimes deer along the way. Let's all look for mountain animals!"

They drove west on I-70, turned off on Colorado Highway 40, and took the winding road up over the Continental Divide at Berthoud Pass. Then they descended slowly, switchback by switchback, into the Grand Valley. They passed Grand Lake and turned in at the west entrance to Rocky Mountain National Park. They stopped at the Kawuneeche Visitor Center to ask directions for a nice, short hike.

To their delight, a park ranger was just about to lead a hike along an easy path. They joined the group, and the ranger led them up the trail. He told them interesting things about the plants, flowers, and animals in the park as well as the history of the place. Occasionally, Hyo translated for Hana, and Su Jin helped the younger kids understand. The whole family enjoyed it.

Hana was entranced by the delicate wildflowers. She thought about how she could add wildflower designs to her pottery. After awhile, the hikers stopped at a group of rocks, and the kids climbed all over them while the ranger told more

34

about the park. Finally, they looped back toward the visitor center. Just as they came near the center, thunder boomed, lightning flashed, and it started to rain. The whole group ran, laughing, into the visitor center.

"This is typical afternoon weather in the Rocky Mountains, folks," said the ranger, cheerfully. "It's best to start your hikes early and come prepared with a rain poncho!"

The Kims ate their picnic at the visitor center and drove back to Denver, feeling relaxed and happy. Unfortunately, the minute they walked in the door, Mother-in-Law started complaining about how long they were gone and nagging Hana to start dinner.

Later, Hana and Hyo got ready for bed. *"Hyo,"* said Hana, *"I think we would be happier if we rented a small apartment of our own. Some of the women in the English class live in a nice apartment complex. It's far from here, but maybe we could find one like it that's closer to the office."*

"Not yet," said Hyo. *"For one thing, Kwan might see it as an insult if we move out so soon after arriving in Denver. Also, we need to save some money. My father left us money to come to the USA, but the move was expensive. Let's try to stay for a year, and then maybe buy a small house."*

Hana agreed, but she didn't know how she could stand a year of Mother-in-Law. She told herself that this was good for her family, which was the most important thing. Still, she wondered when she would be able to resume her pottery.

On Monday, Hyo told Kwan he was going to drive to work.

"In your own car? Why not ride with me?"

"I'm going to a taekwondo studio at 5:00 to work out."

"At 5:00? That's pretty early. I didn't know you were still interested in taekwondo, anyway. I thought you left that behind with your childhood."

Hyo was surprised that Kwan didn't recognize Hyo's accomplishments in taekwondo. He was a master, which took a lot of dedication and hard work. As a young man in Korea, he won awards and top honors in many tournaments. It was unusual for a serious engineering student to compete in a sport, so he was interviewed regularly on television and for magazines. He decided not to argue with Kwan. Today was the day he was going to tell him about the mistake he found in their father's work. He wasn't sure how Kwan would react. He thought Kwan would be happy that he found the error before a disaster happened. But even after talking to Hana, Hyo couldn't be sure he could communicate well with Kwan. Kwan might be angry again.

After lunch, he went into Kwan's office with the plans and his calculations. He explained the mistake to Kwan. Kwan was very angry.

"What were you doing, checking our father's work? I told you to leave these plans alone! You dis-

obeyed me and now we'll have to tell the client that we made a mistake!"

"But Kwan, we found the error in time to fix it with very little cost to anyone. I'll be glad to fix it myself. And I wasn't disobeying you or looking for mistakes! I was just practicing changing Centigrade to Fahrenheit. I wanted to use a real project."

This did not make Kwan happier. "I'm the one who has to call and say we need to send over new plans. And this is father's error. It shames his memory."

"Tell the client your foolish younger brother did it, then," said Hyo, angrily. He turned and walked quickly out of Kwan's office. How could he work with Kwan? Everything Hyo did made Kwan angry or defensive. He never dreamed working with his own brother would be so miserable.

He worked on some minor projects for the afternoon. At 5:00 he turned off his computer and left his office. Kwan was talking to the receptionist in the office waiting area as he walked toward the office door.

Kwan walked quickly to him and took his arm. In a quiet voice, he said, "Hyo, if you start leaving at 5:00 everyone will think it's fine to leave so early. That's why I never leave until after 5:45. You're being a bad example."

"If I stay until 6:00 and then go to taekwondo I won't get home until after 8:00. Hana will be irritated and the kids will be in bed. I don't mind doing that *sometimes, but right now I don't have very much to do. So it seems like a good idea to leave at 5:00."*

Kwan walked out the door with him. *"This is ridiculous. I'm only asking you to stay another 45 minutes or an hour. Is this silly taekwondo worth disobeying me?"*

That was the second time in one day that Kwan used the word "disobey."

"You are my older brother and the senior partner in this company," said Hyo, trying not to be disrespectful, *"but I am not a child. I know about being successful in business. In Korea I worked, practiced taekwondo, and still had time for my family. If I choose to go to taekwondo sometimes, especially if I am not busy, then I don't think you can make me follow your orders."*

"You say you are not a child, but you act like a child!" yelled Kwan. *"Taekwondo is not important for an adult with responsibilities to his family and his job! And this is not Korea. This is the United States of America, and I know what is best in this country."*

Hyo turned and walked toward his car. His brother was yelling at him in public. Probably all the engineers in the office were gathered at the windows watching. It was humiliating.

"You'll have to choose! Taekwondo or the company!" shouted Kwan.

38

Hana's Journal, Monday, September 15

We moved to new apartment last week. It is same place as Sony lives. It is far from this English class but Sony and I can drive together with each other. My husband change work. Now, he is toiling at Korean grocery store. Maybe he will teach at taekwondo gym in evenings. Apartment is nice. We have our family space alone by ourselves.

Karen's Response

Sony and you are carpooling. That will save you money on gas, and you'll have time to become good friends during the drive. How are you feeling about your husband's new job? Is everything OK?

Hana's Journal, Wednesday, September 24

The brother of my husband is angry. His mother is also not happy. She says I am blame for everything. But we think we are maybe more happy now. Grocery store is near to taekwondo gym. We can walk to there from apartment. My husband has dream to have own taekwondo gym. I have dream to resume my pottery work.

Karen's Response

I'm sorry your mother-in-law blames you for all the family's problems. I hope your husband's and your dreams come true. How did your husband learn taekwondo? And how will you find a place to do pottery here?

Sell your books at sellbackyourBook.com!
Go to sellbackyourBook.com
and get an instant price
quote. We even pay the
shipping - see what your old
books are worth today!

00038354060

0003835 4060 S

CHAPTER
❖ 5 ❖

September

Hana, Hyo, and the children settled into a routine. Dak Ho and Cho Hee were enrolled in school. Hana attended her English class three mornings a week. She wanted to find a pottery studio to work in, but her search so far was unsuccessful. She bought a set of colored pencils and sketched some of the wildflowers she had seen in the mountains, and other scenes that caught her eye. She still had time to do the shopping and prepare the dinner every day.

Hyo worked from 8:00 AM to 4:30 PM at the supermarket. Then he went to the taekwondo studio for an hour. It was convenient to live so close to both of them.

One evening, Hyo came home after his workout. He was smiling.

"Tom asked me to teach the Tuesday/Thursday evening intermediate class. I won't be home until after 8:00 those nights, but I told Tom that since it was only two nights a week, it would be alright."

Hyo stopped talking and looked at Hana. Her

41

face showed no reaction. Many thoughts were going through her mind. Her dream of doing pottery again just faded more. But Hyo wanted to do this. The two of them didn't discuss the tension with Kwan now. She knew it bothered him, but she was grateful that he had the supermarket job. It was dull and repetitive, and he was making one-third of the money that he earned as an engineer. It was a great hardship, but they were willing to endure it because they didn't have to put up with Kwan and Mother-in-Law's abuse. But what about their duties to the family? And didn't Hyo deserve to do something that made him happy? Hana weighed these opposing thoughts in her mind.

"I think you should take it," said Hana. *"The children and I will be fine. We'll—"* She was interrupted by the telephone ringing. Hyo answered it.

"Hello . . . *Hello Kwan. How are you and Mother?. . . And Mi Sun and Su Jin? . . . We are all fine, thank you. . . . Yes, I am still working at the grocery store. . . . No, that is not a good idea. . . . I understand."*

Hyo hung up the phone. His face was white. The happiness from a few moments before was gone.

"Hyo . . . ? "

"I can't speak now. I need some time to think. I'll be back later." Hyo left the apartment.

Two hours later, Hana heard Hyo come in the

door. The children were in bed. The TV was on, but Hana couldn't concentrate on the program. She followed her husband into the bedroom. They silently got ready for bed.

"*What happened?*" asked Hana quietly.

"*Kwan said I must come back to the company. He said he might report me to Immigration if I don't. The H-1B visa that I have is for professionals. He said he is the sponsoring employer, and that I must work as a professional at the company. The supermarket is not a professional workplace, so I can't apply for a new H-1B visa with them.*"

"*We have no choice, then,*" said Hana. "*I do not want to get in trouble with the American government, and I don't want to be here illegally.*"

"*I don't want to either, but I cannot go back to work with Kwan. Maybe there is another way. We can look it up on the Internet. Maybe you can get a visa as a special artist. We have a few days since, technically, I am still on a short leave from the company.*"

Hana rubbed his back. She could feel him relaxing under her fingers. She said, "*It seemed like we were doing the right thing when we came here to help your brother. Now we're barely speaking to Kwan, Mother-in-Law is mad at us, and you're working in a supermarket. This is our worst nightmare. It's not how I wanted it to be.*"

"*Do you think I wanted this to happen?*" asked Hyo. His muscles were tensing up again. "*We had*

43

a pretty good life in Korea. I was a respected tae-kwondo master and a good engineer. It's not what I pictured either."

"Oh, Hyo, maybe we should go back!"

"How? We have so little money saved. Would we be better off there than here?"

"I don't know. I can't think straight. There is no more we can do tonight. Let's try to get some sleep," said Hana, knowing she would be awake for hours.

Hana and Sony talked quietly with two other students in their English class during their break. One was from Morocco and Maria was Mexican, so the conversation was in English.

"You like you new apartment, Hana?" asked Maria.

"Yes but is small. My son and daughter sleep by same room."

"My daughters, too. They no like, but I say, 'Stop crying. Is okay for now,'" said Maria.

Karen, their teacher, interrupted their conversation.

"Let's get started." The students took their seats.

"Today we're going to start a new project. We'll try doing some watercolor painting and then write poetry to go with the pictures. Then you'll each make a book of your pictures. This is Linda's idea," Karen said. She motioned to Linda, a volunteer who worked in the class once a week. "Linda, do you want to explain it in more detail?"

"Okay," answered Linda. She was tall and slender with long, straight auburn hair. It was pulled back and tied in a ponytail with a pretty scarf in shades of purple that contrasted with her yellow and green top.

"I learned about this at a workshop I went to last month. It's fun and easy, and I thought you would like it, too. I'll teach the painting. Karen will work on the writing with you. You'll be writing poems that describe your pictures, which will help you expand your vocabulary."

Linda showed them the book she made. It was called *Summer Flowers*. Linda had painted pictures of the same garden in different months to show the changes from May to September. It was beautiful.

"I no can paint like that," said Maria.

Karen laughed. "Neither can I. Linda is an artist. Some of you went to her show last year, remember? But she helped me. These are the pictures I drew using this process. And I'm definitely not an artist," she said as she held up her paintings. The students could see that the pictures were not professional, but Karen used pleasing colors that helped show the differences in her garden from month to month.

"The painting is just the first part of the project.

45

In a few weeks after we finish the painting, we will write the poems. Linda, can you tell the students what to do to get started?"

Linda laid out all the supplies she needed to model the first step. The students spread newspaper on their tables. Then they got squares of watercolor paper, brushes, paints, and containers with water.

The morning passed quickly for Hana. The brush in her hand moved as if she had been painting watercolor for years.

"That is beautiful. I didn't know you were a painter. I thought you said you were a potter," said Sony.

"Look, Karen. Now we have two artist, Linda and Hana," said Maria.

Hana looked up. Her face turned pink from all the attention. Linda said, "Are you a painter, Hana?"

"No, I am potter. In Korea, I make vase and bowl, not picture."

"Well, I agree with Maria. You are an artist."

For the first time in weeks, Hana felt hopeful about her art. Maybe she couldn't do pottery now, but she was able to express herself through painting.

At the end of class, Linda told everyone about an art show and sale the next weekend. It was an end-of-the-summer tradition. A couple of streets near an art school were closed to traffic. Art students and area artists set up booths to display their work. Several classmates were interested and made plans to go together. Hana thought her family and possibly Mi Sun would like to go, too. With the tensions between Hyo and Kwan, and between her and her mother-in-law, Hana didn't have many opportunities to see Mi Sun. Hyo and Kwan were not getting along, but the two wives were still good friends. They talked to each other often.

That weekend, Hana went with Sony to the art show. The children, Hyo, and Mi Sun were busy with other plans. The streets were crowded with people all looking at the art at each booth. Paintings hung on the walls and filled bins in many of the booths. Jewelers displayed their necklaces and rings in glass cases. Potters had their work out on shelves.

The two women wandered from one end of the show to the other, looking at everything, and stopping occasionally for a closer look at something. Sony found some jewelry that she liked and finally bought a pretty silver necklace.

Hana was interested in the pottery. She didn't want to buy anything, but she wanted to know where the artists worked. The pots in one booth looked like they were made by students.

"Can I help you?" asked a young man.

47

"Yes. Where you make pottery?" said Hana.

"Right here at the art school. There are beginning and intermediate classes, and students get to use the potters wheels during free periods. Here's a schedule. The classes fill up quickly, so sign up early."

Hana took the schedule and thanked the man.

"Do you want to take classes?" asked Sony.

"No, but I want to find someplace to work on my own."

"Hi, Sony. Hi, Hana. Great to see you here!"

Surprised, the women turned to see Linda in the next booth.

"How do you like the show?" asked Linda.

"Is very good, but so many people!" said Sony.

"And very hot," added Hana.

"At least it isn't raining," said Linda. "Last year there was a big thunderstorm in the afternoon. It was crazy! Everyone was trying to protect the art and not get wet at the same time."

"You have paintings here?" asked Hana.

"Yes, a few. Most of my work is in a gallery downtown. But here are some paintings I did in Santa Fe."

Hana expected to see watercolors of adobe houses with blue doors and bright flowers. She was surprised to see abstract paintings of browns, blues, and reds.

"Oh! You not paint like in class?"

"No, not usually. I like to be in a place and get

the feel of it. Then I paint my feelings, not real objects or places."

"When, uh, where you paint?" asked Hana.

"Where do I paint? My studio is a room in my apartment."

Sony said, "Hana is looking for pottery workplace. Do you know place?"

"You're looking for a studio? Hmmm. Maybe. I have a friend who is a potter. I'll ask her and tell you in class, okay?"

"Really? Okay. See you Monday."

During the break in class on Monday, Linda came up to Hana. She handed her a piece of paper with a name and phone number on it.

"This is my friend that I told you about. You can call her. She said she is in a co-op." She explained that six or seven potters rented a building together. They all had space to work and a kiln to fire their pots.

"Oh, thank you. But is very difficult for me to talk with phone. You can . . . ?"

"Can I call her for you?" laughed Linda. "Of course. But even better, we can go there and see it and meet my friend. How about that?"

"Yes?"

"Yes. Can you go on Wednesday after class?"

"I not drive."

"No problem. I'll drive. And I'll take you home afterward."

49

❖

The phone was ringing as Hana let herself into the apartment on Wednesday afternoon. It was Mi Sun.

"Oh, Mi Sun! I am so excited. Linda, the volunteer in my English class, just took me to a pottery studio. One of the members is moving, and I can take her place. I have missed doing pottery so much! And Linda invited me to go to an art show opening on Friday. She has two paintings in it. Hyo can take care of the kids since it is at night."

Mi Sun was silent for a moment. Then she said, *"Hana, be careful. This friendship happened very quickly. Linda is an American. Americans can seem friendly to your face, but are the opposite behind your back. And most important, they have different values. Often they don't take their family responsibilities seriously. Do you know about her family? Is she married? Is she a good daughter? Also, Americans are very individualistic. They are the most important ones, not their families. You already have problems to deal with. Do not let Mother-in-Law be right about you."*

CHAPTER
❖ 6 ❖

September

Hana listened carefully to Mi Sun. After she hung up, she sat and thought about her. She seemed happy here in America, but was she really? She didn't have very many American friends. Her friends were Korean women from her church. At home, Mother-in-Law always told her what to do. And Kwan didn't seem to think her job was important. Mi Sun still did all the cooking and cleaning, even though she and Kwan both worked.

Then Hana realized she herself also did all the housework, even in Korea when she was working. Here, Sony, a Korean, was becoming Hana's good friend. She was not so different from Mi Sun. To be honest, she liked Mi Sun and admired the way she kept her home harmonious. Maybe there was some truth to what Mi Sun said. Maybe she didn't have very many American friends because it was difficult to become close to a person with different values.

Hana decided to continue being friends with Linda, but to keep Mi Sun's words in mind. She really hoped she could join the pottery co-op. If she did, she would be careful about how close she got to Linda and the other women there.

❖

Later that day, Hyo finished his work at the supermarket. He went next door to exercise at the taekwondo studio. Tom saw him come in and greeted him.

"You got a few minutes? There's something I want to talk to you about," said Tom.

The two men went into the back of the studio, where Tom had a large office.

"Please sit down," said Tom, switching from English to Korean. *"Would you like some tea?"*

"Yes, thanks," said Hyo.

Hyo and Tom often had a cup of tea before a workout, and sometimes a beer afterward. They liked each other, and liked to talk about the studio, the students, and martial arts. When Hyo quit his job with Kwan, he told Tom all about it. Tom understood how hard Hyo found it to take orders from his brother. He knew that Hyo didn't like working at the supermarket, but that it was a temporary way to support his family.

Hyo sipped from his steaming cup. *"How are things going?"*

"Hyo, they're going well. Very well. In fact, I'm thinking about expanding the studio. The space next door is vacant. I could take it over. I was thinking of creating a sparring ring and another classroom."

Hyo felt happy for his friend. But he also felt a little jealous. Tom had a nice studio, with a growing list of students. He was spending his life doing something he loved. He had no boss but himself. Hyo was stuck between working for his brother and a dead-end supermarket job.

"That's great," said Hyo. "I know you'll do a good job with it."

"It's a lot for me to take on by myself," said Tom. "I was thinking of adding a partner."

"Oh? Really?"

"Well, you've only been here about a month, but I like to follow my instincts about people. It seems to me that with your work ethic and your mastery of taekwondo, you would make a good partner."

Hyo was stunned. "This is quite a surprise," he said. "I don't quite know what to think. Maybe if you tell me a little more—." He stopped. He wasn't even sure what kind of questions to ask.

"Well, I was thinking you might like to work here with me full time and even invest in the business. Frankly, eventually I'd like to open several studios around town. You're Korean, so you would add authenticity to my business. The fact that you're fluent in English is also a plus. Let me show you some figures I've been working on."

Hyo's mind was buzzing. As he looked at the financial spreadsheets Tom had created, he got more and more excited. Tom had a good plan worked out. The costs for renting and renovating the new space and for Hyo's salary seemed reasonable. The increase in the number of students

53

seemed realistic. Hyo began to think this might be possible.

Then he had another thought. This might be his way out of his visa problems, too. Maybe Tom could apply for the H-1B visa for him. Hyo was a Korean taekwondo expert. He was essential to the expansion of the business.

He and Tom talked for more than an hour. As they discussed the plans, Hyo realized that Tom wanted an equal partner. He asked Hyo for his opinion on several options. He pulled the spreadsheet up on the computer, and the two men began to make some changes together.

Finally, Hyo said, *"I'll do it. I don't have a lot of money to invest, but I can give you my time."*

Tom smiled. He held out his hand and Hyo shook it. *"We can work all that out over the next couple of weeks. The first thing we have to do is negotiate a favorable lease for the new space. I'll call the property manager tomorrow."*

Hyo looked around Tom's office. It was large, big enough for one desk, but it was very cluttered. It looked disorganized.

"I have an idea," he said. *"With all the new students and extra scheduling, we'll need an office manager. But, we can't afford anyone at first. What do you think of Hana helping out in here?"*

"Would she want to?"

"Sure! She's not working. She's just taking some English classes. I know she would be good at orga-

nizing all this," he waved his hand at the messy room. *"And she's an artist. Maybe she could help with advertising, too."*

"We'll make it a family business," said Tom. He laughed, and Hyo laughed with him.

After his talk with Tom, Hyo worked out. Then he and Tom talked some more. He told Tom that Kwan wanted him to return to the engineering firm and about the visa problem. They researched work visas on the Internet. Finally, at 10:00 PM, the men locked up the studio and said goodbye. Hyo almost felt like he was already working full time at the studio, as Tom's partner.

Hana was in bed when Hyo got home. He tried to be very quiet. As he hung up his trousers, his change fell out of his pocket onto the floor, jingling and clinking.

"Hyo! Is that you?" asked Hana, sleepily.

"Were you expecting someone else?" he teased her.

Hana reached over and turned on the bedside lamp. *"Did you teach tonight? It's only Wednesday."*

Really, Hyo was glad she was awake, because he wanted to tell her about his day.

"No, I didn't teach. But Tom and I had a very interesting talk."

He emptied his trouser pockets of the rest of their contents. Then, he got into bed and told Hana all about Tom's offer. Hana listened quietly.

55

Then he said, *"And, I got you a job, too. It's not paid in money, but I think Tom will apply your time toward our investment in the business."*

Hana sat up. She propped her pillow up against the bed's headboard. *"Are you sure you want to do this?"*

"I know it's sudden, but yes. When Tom and I were talking I realized this must be the reason we came to the U.S. In Korea, I would have worked as an engineer my whole life. Now, with hard work, I can do something I love and build a successful business."

Hana understood. In Korea, for Hyo, taekwondo was a hobby. It wasn't a serious profession for a grown man. Here, he could take that hobby and make it his life.

Oh, yes, she understood. She loved Hyo, and she wanted him to be happy. But Hyo was offering her services to the business as well. She knew that if she worked in the taekwondo studio she wouldn't have time for her art. She didn't want to give up pottery. Was that selfish? If Hyo was successful, he thought he could make a lot of money. Then the family would be secure.

"Hyo, if we do this, we're saying we want to stay in the USA. Is that what you want?" she asked.

"I think so. I don't think I would get this opportunity in Korea. My father wouldn't let me go to a

56

sports school. In Korea, I'm not considered an expert. Here, I am."

Hana decided now was not the time to tell Hyo about her conversation with Mi Sun. Instead, she said, *"What about Kwan? He expects you to rejoin the engineering company."*

For the first time, Hyo looked troubled. *"I know. I wish I could be friends with him, make him understand why I don't want to work with him."*

"He's not going to understand, though. To him, it will look like you're picking partnership with Tom, an American you barely know, over your own brother."

"I know," said Hyo.

"How will you persuade him to switch your visa to Tom's business? I wonder if you can do that," said Hana.

"Tom and I found some information about an EB-1 visa. We printed this from the Internet." He reached over to the bedside table and got a piece of paper. He gave it to Hana, who read it. It was in English, and very difficult.

"I'm sorry Hyo. I can't really understand this. It's a little too hard."

"Well, basically it says that people who are top experts can get permanent visas to work in the USA. Athletes are included. Tom and I think that I might qualify as a taekwondo expert."

"Oh, well, that sounds good," said Hana. She

57

was starting to feel very sleepy. It was past midnight. It seemed like all their important conversations were happening late at night. *"Honey, can we talk in the morning?"*

Hyo pulled her to him and kissed her. *"Of course,"* he said. *"No more talking now."*

The next morning, Hyo looked like he had slept for 12 hours. His eyes were bright, and he sang a silly song to the children as they came into the kitchen for breakfast. Hana knew she did not look as good. She had slept well, but it seemed like only minutes passed between the time she went to sleep and the alarm clock's shrill ring.

The kids giggled at their silly daddy. Then Hyo said, *"Do you kids remember when we went to see the Korean Tigers Taekwondo Club perform in Seoul?"*

"Oh, yeah," grinned Dak Ho. *"They were amazing! Remember, they did forms to music, and showed how to kick and punch, and remember that guy who was shaking his hands at that other guy, and then the first guy started shaking all over—"*

Cho Hee joined in: *"I remember the flips! They all did lots of flips!"*

"Yes, that's right!" said Hyo. He was enjoying the kids' enthusiasm. *"We're going to start a new taekwondo business. Maybe you two can help out. And do you want to take classes?"*

Both the kids were delighted. Hana was tired,

and not sure she wanted to encourage this new taekwondo business, but she had to smile. When Hyo was in a good mood, everyone was in a good mood. The kids were already agreeing to work at the studio. This would be good for the family. How could she be the one to stand in the way?

CHAPTER
❖ 7 ❖

Early October

Karen, Hana's English teacher, stood at the front of the classroom. On the board was a calendar grid for the month of October. She and the students discussed plans for the topics they would cover for the month, including specific questions and information they wanted to address.

"Okay, we'll be talking about fall and changes we experience at this time of year and in our lives. Of course we'll discuss Halloween. And we'll continue with our painting and poetry for our books, and book club and our interactive journals. Is there anything else you'd like to talk about this month?

Hana raised her hand.

"Yes, Hana?"

"My children has . . . have report card. I must talk with teacher next week. What can I say?"

"Ah, you have teacher conferences. How many of you have children in school?" she asked the class. Most of the students raised their hands. "So this is important for a lot of you. We'll address it in our next class. We can do some role playing. But let's start talking about it now. We have ten minutes before class is over. What do you want to know? What do you want to ask or tell the teacher? What do you think the teacher will ask you?"

Maria spoke. "My daughter have English class?"

"Okay. 'Does my daughter go to a class for English language learners?' or 'Does my daughter have an English class?'" Karen wrote the sentences on the board. "What else?"

"I have only baby now, but she . . . grow. What does she study?" said Sony.

"Good question, Sony. 'What is my child's schedule?' or 'What is Dak Ho studying or learning?' How else could you ask about this?"

Several students and Linda offered suggestions. When class was over, Linda went up to Hana as she was putting her notebook into her bag.

"Hey Hana. Do you have a minute? I wanted to tell you that my friend called me from the pottery co-op. She wants to know if you're going to take the space or not."

"Oh, Linda. I want it, but now I not sure."

"Why? Tell me about it. Maybe I can help you figure something out," said Linda.

Hana looked at Sony who was waiting for her. "I must leave. Sony is driver."

"I can take you home."

Hana felt confused. She looked at Sony, who looked back at her. Hana had told Sony a little about her situation, about wanting to do pottery again, but not all her feelings or very many specifics about the problems between Hyo and Kwan. She kept that information private out of respect for her family.

Linda continued, "I have an appointment in an hour, so I only have a little while to talk about this. My friend really needs to know your decision soon. Today, if you can. There is someone else who is interested in taking the space if you don't want it."

"Okay," said Hana. "I will go with you now." She turned to Sony. *"Sorry, Sony. I'd better take care of this now. I'll see you Wednesday."*

Sony said goodbye and left. Everyone else had left the room, too. The two women sat down.

"So, what's going on? I thought you really wanted to do pottery here. This seems like the perfect solution," said Linda.

"Yes, but everything very complicated now."

"Why? What happened?"

Mi Sun's words were ringing in Hana's ears. She needed to be careful with Linda. But Hana could sense that Linda was not the kind of person that Mi Sun was warning her about. Yes, she was American. But not all Americans fit the stereotype.

"My husband change job. Now he work . . . works in grocery store and in taekwondo gym."

"Yes, I know. I read your journal entry last week."

"So now I will work in taekwondo gym, too."

"But Hana, what about your art? This is a great

opportunity for you! I haven't seen any of your pottery, but I know you are a good artist. You can't just give it up!"

"I . . . I—"

"Listen, Hana. You are gifted. I know from my own experience that I must paint. And I think you must do pottery, too."

"It is not simple decision. I must consider my family. But maybe . . . "

Linda saw that Hana was torn. "How about I call my friend and ask for a few more days to decide for sure. You can think about it. This opportunity might not come again. I think you will regret it if you say no. We are a lot alike, Hana."

On Thursday, Hana stood outside room 211 at her children's school. She could see that the teacher was still talking to another parent. She felt nervous. Would she understand the teacher? Would she remember what she learned in class about talking to a teacher at parent conferences?

"Hello. You must be Dak Ho's mother. I'm Ms. Johnson. Come sit down." The two women shook hands.

"Let me show you some of Dak Ho's work. He's doing very well in math. Here are his papers. As you can see, his work is very neat."

"Ah, yes. He is careful like father."

63

"Oh? What does your husband do?"

"He is engineer."

"Oh, I see. Let me show you Dak Ho's work in his other subjects. We did an in-class project in science. Here is the report from his group. They did very well. He got full points for everything, even participation. He talks more with his friends than he does in the whole class."

"Really? He is speaking English?" asked Hana.

"Yes, of course. There are no other Korean speakers in the class. And he goes to Mr. O'Donnell's class for extra English help."

"Mr. O'Donnell?"

"Yes. I'm surprised that Dak Ho hasn't told you about him. He's great. The kids call him Mr. O. He's here today if you want to talk to him."

"Ah, Mr. O. Dak Ho say . . . says he is very nice."

Hana stayed for a few more minutes and asked some questions that she had practiced in her English class. She understood most of what Ms. Johnson said. Then she went to Mr. O's room. He was sitting at his desk working on the computer, but came to greet Hana when she entered the room. He was very tall. He had an easy smile and a handsome, youthful face.

"Mr. O? I am the mother of Dak Ho and Cho Hee."

"Yes, of course. Nice to meet you. Thank you for stopping by. I work with both of your children here every day. Let me tell you about my program. Cho Hee comes with five other first graders. We're working on descriptions, and use these Attribute Cards with all sorts of topics. She catches on quickly. So does Dak Ho." He paused. "I'm glad you're here."

Hana felt pleased. "Thank you," she said.

Mr. O asked her to sit down. Then he said, "I was wondering if something happened at school or at home that would explain why Dak Ho's behavior has changed. About three weeks ago, he became quiet and sullen. He—"

"Sullen? I'm sorry. I don't understand."

"When he first came to class, he was friendly and outgoing, not shy at all. But then he stopped participating in our discussions. He still played games and did his work, but he stopped talking. Did something happen at home?"

Hana was unsure what to say. "We moved to apartment, and . . . "

"That must be it. Then today, out of the blue, he started playing around with the other kids and doing karate moves."

"Taekwondo. My husband has black belt. Dak Ho takes classes."

"That explains a lot. Change is hard, and moving is a big change. Say, do you think your husband would be willing to come in sometime and give a demonstration?"

"I will ask."

65

❖

Hana felt low after the conferences. The reports of her children were positive, but Dak Ho's behavior in Mr. O's class troubled her. She didn't think his behavior was caused by the move. She felt sure that the situation between Hyo and Kwan was the real reason. She and Hyo didn't talk about it in front of the children, but she knew they sensed something important was wrong.

Then Hana thought about her art dilemma. She wanted to talk to someone and get another perspective. She couldn't ask Mi Sun. Hana hadn't yet told her about Hyo's new business idea and the job he wanted her to do. Besides, she knew what Mi Sun would say. Mi Sun would tell her that she must do as Hyo asks because this is what is best for the family. She must do the job in the taekwondo studio and forget about doing pottery. The family needed her, and that was her role. It was selfish to do what she wanted.

Hana became more depressed. She lay down on the couch for a nap. Thoughts were swirling in her mind. *This is crazy,* she said to herself. *I can't rest. Maybe if I get up and write down these thoughts, it will be clear to me what I should do.*

Hana found some paper and started to write in Korean.

What should I do about the pottery co-op? I am so confused. Linda says I must do my art. Mi Sun

66

*does not agree. That is not the Korean way. I must put family first. But I am an artist **and** I am a Korean woman. Deep inside, I will not be completely happy no matter which one I choose. Maybe that is self-centered and selfish. I wish I could talk to Hyo about this. But he is on fire, so excited about the taekwondo studio. Also, I don't want to burden him with one more thing. The bad relationship with his brother weighs him down enough. In Korea, he was content and worked as an engineer while I pursued pottery. And he did taekwondo. Is it his turn now for his dream to come true? I can't expect him to continue to work at the grocery store while I do pottery. And working with Kwan is impossible. He deserves to be happy. But is this the best path for the family? I don't want to work at the studio office organizing and advertising. And what about the children? Cho Hee seems fine, but I'm worried about Dak Ho. No matter what I do, Mother-in-Law will find something wrong with me and my decision.*

That thought made Hana feel worse. She put her head down on her arms on the table and began to cry.

CHAPTER
❖ 8 ❖

Mid-October

Hyo stood at the door to the taekwondo studio. He was saying goodbye to his students. Soon, they were all gone. He went into the office. He and Tom had the habit of talking over progress on their plans after the last class. Hyo liked this time with Tom, seeing their dream come to life, little by little.

Suddenly, the doorbell rang, indicating that someone was in the studio.

"I guess I forgot to lock the door," said Hyo. "I'll go see who it is."

When he entered the studio, he was surprised to see who was standing in the middle of the room.

"*Kwan!*" he said.

"*Hello, Hyo.*" He looked around the room. "*So this is where you work now?*"

"*Yes. I'm investing in Tom's company.*"

Kwan walked over to the door to one of the smaller classrooms and looked in. Then he turned and faced Hyo. "*I've come to tell you that you have made a mistake. This is not the place for you. You absolutely must not invest in this business. You're a professional, not an exercise instructor.*"

Hyo felt every word like a punch in the stomach. He tried to stay calm. He did not want to speak in anger.

"I'm sorry you feel that way," he said. *"But I don't think I'm just an exercise instructor."*

What more could he say to his brother? Nothing would help.

"Our father wanted us to continue in the field he chose for us. We are engineers. People respect us because we are professionals. This is a job with no respect. Anyone can do it," said Kwan.

Hyo was speechless. His silence irritated Kwan. *"You don't even know why you're doing this! You can't defend it! This is not why Father left you money to move here. I should have your work visa revoked."*

Hyo closed his eyes and chose his words carefully. *"I worked hard to get into a good university and become an engineer, that's true. But I also worked hard for many years to get my fifth-degree black belt."* He opened his eyes. Suddenly, he knew what to say. *"Our father was proud of that. He supported all my efforts to practice and compete."*

Kwan's face was red and he was frowning, but he was listening carefully. Before Kwan spoke, Tom came out of the office.

"Oh, hello," he said. He smiled in his friendly way.

Kwan nodded his head.

"Tom, this is my brother, Kwan Kim. He has come to see my investment."

69

Kwan nodded again. Tom put out his hand, and Kwan shook it.

"Good to meet you," said Tom.

"Nice to meet you, too," said Kwan.

Hyo was happy that Kwan was being polite. He wasn't going to embarrass Hyo by saying anything about their disagreement.

Tom switched to Korean. *"Would you like me to show you around the studio?"*

"Oh, your Korean is very good," said Kwan. *"Where did you learn?"*

Tom explained how he had learned to speak Korean. Then Kwan said, *"Thank you for your offer, but I'll have to come back another time. It's getting late and I should go home."* He turned to Hyo. *"Let's talk more about this later."*

"Yes," said Hyo. *"I'll visit you at your house soon."*

Kwan left. Tom and Hyo turned off the lights to the studio, locked the doors, and left.

Later, at home, Hyo and Hana sat in the small apartment kitchen and had a cup of tea. Hyo told Hana about Kwan's visit to the studio. *"I kept my composure,"* he said. *"And, as I was telling Kwan that Father was proud of my taekwondo skills, I realized that was really true. One reason I tried so hard was because Father supported me. Maybe he would think investing in the studio is not such a bad idea."*

Hana nodded. *"It's possible,"* she said.

Hyo reached over and covered Hana's hand

70

with his. *"We can use your help right away at the studio. Can you come tomorrow?"*

Hana hoped her emotions did not show on her face. *"Of course,"* she said. *"But let's agree that I will continue my English classes, too. So I'll walk over after my class tomorrow."*

"That's fine," said Hyo. He leaned over and kissed her. *"I think things are going to be alright."*

Hana nodded again and smiled. She didn't know if things would be alright, but she did like to see Hyo happy.

The next day, early in the morning, Hana called Mi Sun.

"Can I come over this morning?" she asked.

"That would be lovely, but I have to go to work," said Mi Sun. *"Is something wrong?"*

"How was Kwan acting after he visited the tae-kwondo studio last night?" asked Hana.

"Strange," said Mi Sun. *"He didn't want to talk about it. He seemed a little angry, but mostly sad."*

"Really? Sad?"

"Yes. What did Hyo say to him?"

"That's what I want to talk about," said Hana.

"Okay, I'll call in to work and say that I'll be late. When can you be here?"

"I'll get a ride with Sony, so I can be there by about 8:30."

71

When Hana arrived, Mi Sun and Mother-in-Law were waiting for her.

"Mi Sun told me you two are going to talk about my sons," said Mother-in-Law.

"Yes, we are worried. We want them to behave like brothers, not enemies," said Hana.

"Tell me what you wanted to tell Mi Sun."

Hana told both women that Hyo thought that his father would approve of Hyo working in a taekwondo studio. "Father-in-Law always supported Hyo's hard work in taekwondo. And he was proud of how smart Hyo was. Father-in-Law was proud that Hyo could be so good at taekwondo and also go to such a good university and get an engineering degree. Hyo thinks Father-in-Law would support him in this decision now."

"Maybe," said Mother-in-Law, "but my husband wouldn't want Hyo to abandon his brother at this time. Kwan took on new projects because he thought Hyo would be a big help. And Kwan is so disappointed. Before you came to the U.S., he talked a lot about how great it would be to have Hyo by his side."

"Mother-in-Law, how can we help these brothers be friends? We are a family. What can we do?"

The three women talked for a little while more. Mother-in-Law said, "The only solution is for Hyo to go back to work with Kwan. Kwan is the older brother. It is Hyo's place to respect him. You two are their wives. You must help make this happen. Hana, *talk to Hyo. Mi Sun, tell Kwan to let Hyo come back without humiliating him."*

Hana thought that Mother-in-Law was right. She didn't know how she was going to persuade Hyo of it. Then it was time for Hana to go to English class and for Mi Sun to go to work. Mother-in-Law walked to the door with them.

"I want peace between my sons. You two are responsible," she said.

At school, Hana wrote in her journal:

I went to teacher conference and I said some questions we learned. I understand everything the teachers say. I am happy about that understanding. I am little worried about my son. He studies well, but he plays taekwondo in school. Teacher did not want that. Do you have children? Do you ever go to teacher conference?

Karen often asked Hana questions in her responses to Hana's journal. This was the first time Hana had asked questions in her journal to Karen. Hana thought the journal would be a good place to ask an American mother for advice.

After she underlined some mistakes in Hana's writing, Karen wrote back:

73

Karen's Response

Yes, I have two children, a boy and a girl. But they are both in college now! I went to teacher conferences for many years. Sometimes the teachers said nice things about my children. And sometimes the teachers complained that they didn't always behave. What did your son's teacher say?

Hana knew what she would write back. She would tell Karen that Dak Ho wasn't talking as much as before. Maybe Karen would have some advice about what to say to Dak Ho. She might have some ideas about how to get him to speak more in class again.

She told Sony that she was going to work in the taekwondo studio. Sony took her there instead of to her apartment. Hyo was pleased to see her come in so early. He showed her the office and suggested how she could get started organizing things.

Soon Tom came in, greeted her, and put on some Korean pop music. She spent the afternoon working with him to develop a good system for keeping track of student information. She was surprised to find that she was good at it. She understood what he wanted quickly and had simple solutions to some of his problems.

Before she knew it, it was time to pick up the children from school.

Later, as she prepared dinner, the doorbell rang. She hurried to open the door. Dak Ho and Cho Hee went, too. They were excited by visitors.

It was Mi Sun.

"Did you bring Su Jin?" they asked. They looked behind her for their cousin.

"Not this time. But she sent you this! You can't have it, but she said you can borrow it for a while." She handed them a video game.

"Oh, wow! Can we play this now? Please?" asked Dak Ho.

Hana smiled. *"Is your homework done?"*

"All done," said the kids, together.

"Go ahead."

Hana gestured for Mi Sun to come in. The women went into the kitchen.

"I've been thinking all day," said Mi Sun. *"I came here from work instead of going home. Mother-in-Law will wonder where I am!"*

The two women laughed and sat down.

"I've been thinking, too," said Hana. *"And I have an idea."*

"Tell me!" said Mi Sun.

"Today I worked at the taekwondo studio all afternoon. Tom helped me until it was time for me to pick up the kids from school. Mi Sun, I realized all the classes are in the late afternoon and evening. I won-

75

der if Kwan would think about asking Hyo to work from about 8:00 to 2:00 every day for the next six months. By that time, they can finish up the biggest projects and Kwan will have time to find someone else to work with him."

Mi Sun nodded slowly. "Hmm. Do you think Hyo would do it?"

"I can think of two reasons to do it. One is that he wants harmony in the family, too. The other is that he can invest more money in the business if Kwan will pay him a part-time salary. But Kwan will have to give him some real work to do."

Mi Sun sighed. "Kwan is so stubborn. He says he needs Hyo by his side, but he won't give up any responsibility. Also, I don't think he'll ask Hyo to come back again."

"Ask?" Hana laughed. "He never asked; he demanded!"

Mi Sun laughed, too. "Well, for Kwan to go to the studio was like begging in his opinion."

"Okay," said Hana. "I'll persuade Hyo to offer to help."

"Really? Do you think he will?"

"Maybe. He wants to please Mother-in-Law and Kwan. But do you think you can convince Kwan to agree to give him some real work?"

Mi Sun shrugged her shoulders. "It's worth a try. We all want a happy family."

Mi Sun left and Hana continued to fix dinner. She felt quite good. She was surprised at how calm she felt. She didn't hate working in the office, as she thought she would. In fact, it was satisfying to organize and solve the studio's problems. Soon, she would not need to spend every day there. She could develop systems that just needed to be maintained.

She thought that the plan she and Mi Sun talked about to bring Hyo and Kwan together might work. If it did, Mother-in-Law might be nicer to her. Then, with the family harmony restored, she might find time for her art.

CHAPTER

❖ 9 ❖

Late October

The red and yellow leaves on the trees were brilliant against the bright blue sky. Hana looked at them out the car window as she drove home from English class with Sony.

"The leaves are so beautiful! It's easy to forget all my troubles on a beautiful day like today," said Hana. *"I want to go home and paint them. But today's my day to work at the taekwondo studio. You can drop me there, okay?"*

"Sure. What troubles do you have? I thought everything was going well for you since you moved into your own apartment," said Sony.

"Well, it is much better for me because I don't see my mother-in-law every day." The two women smiled at each other.

"But . . . " Hana hesitated. She thought of her conversation with Mi Sun and their decision to try to get the brothers to be friends again. She was hoping to talk to Hyo tonight. She didn't want to tell Sony about that, but she decided she could tell her part of their troubles.

"Now that Hyo is becoming a partner in the tae-

78

kwondo studio, we don't have extra money. The kids get to take lessons free, but we can't save anything. I worry about it."

"What about your pottery? Could you make some and sell some?"

Hana sighed. "I didn't join the co-op. Hyo needs me to help at the taekwondo studio. And I want to continue English classes. I miss pottery, but I have to have several hours at a time to do it. It doesn't matter now. I already told Linda my answer was no. She was disappointed."

"Linda can work on her art full time. She's single. Maybe she doesn't understand how much time it takes to take care of a family."

"Hmm. That's what my sister-in-law said. Well, thanks for the ride." Hana got out of the car and waved goodbye to Sony.

It was quiet in the studio. Hana turned on the lights in the office. She looked around. The bills were paid and the student files all organized, so she turned her attention to decorating. The room was small and rectangular. Hana had already painted the studio office walls. They were a light, soothing green. Now she moved the furniture around until she was satisfied. She put the desk in the corner facing the door, so she could greet anyone who entered. The blue couch was along one wall. Two simple but comfortable blue chairs and wooden end tables were along another wall. Hana placed a lush green plant on the corner of the desk. She put another one on one of the tables. She put a lamp beside the couch. Then, she stood in the doorway to look at the room.

Hyo came up behind her. He looked over her shoulder. *"It's very nice, Hana,"* he said. *"You did a beautiful job, even with this small space."*

"Thank you, Hyo. It's not quite finished yet. Something is missing, but I'm not sure what it is. I want to put up some pictures and get some bright pillows. Maybe that's it."

"That's probably what it needs. Have you seen Tom?"

"No. I've been alone here all afternoon. It's time for me to go pick up the kids. You have class soon, don't you?"

"Yes," answered Hyo. *"I'll be home around 8."*

"Okay. I'll see you later then. I have an idea I want to talk to you about," said Hana. She said goodbye and left.

Hyo looked at his watch. Students would be coming in about 15 minutes. Tom was always in his uniform, warming up by this time. Where was he? Hyo was the assistant in this class. Tom always opened the session with the students standing at attention, facing him. Hyo put on his uniform, unlocked the doors, and went into the studio to welcome the students.

In the middle of the third exercise, Tom arrived. He looked in the room, nodded to Hyo, and then disappeared. Several minutes later, he reappeared wearing his uniform and joined the class.

After class, Hyo spoke to Tom.

"Is everything alright? You look tired."

"I'm sorry I was late. I was talking to some of the other shop owners. This afternoon, we all got an email from a national leasing company. Read this, Hyo."

Tom handed Hyo a printed copy of the email.

This email is to inform you that we have just bought out the company that leases all the spaces for the businesses in this strip mall. There will be a meeting of the tenants with a representative from our company on October 26, at 7:30 PM.

Hyo looked up at Tom. *"That's tonight."*

"Yes. I'm going. I can tell you about it tomorrow."

"I would like to come, too."

It was almost 9 PM when Hyo came home. Hana sensed that something was wrong.

"Hyo—"

Hyo held up his hand. *"Are the kids in bed?"*

"Yes."

"I'll tell them goodnight."

When he returned, Hyo took a deep breath and let it out. He told Hana about the email and the meeting.

81

"What does that mean for the business?" asked Hana.

"They're raising the rent. It's so expensive, we'll have trouble paying it every month. And expanding now is impossible. Tom had two investors, but with the news of the buyout, one of them is probably going to back out. All our plans and dreams are ruined."

Hana sat quietly, thinking. She paid the bills for the studio, but she didn't know the financial details of the expansion plans. If Hyo went back to work for Kwan part time, could he make enough money to invest in the company himself? With this upsetting news, would Hyo even consider asking Kwan to take him back?

Hyo continued, *"That's enough bad news for one day. This afternoon you said you had something to talk about. What is it? I hope it's good news."*

"It can wait until tomorrow." Hana rubbed Hyo's shoulders.

"What? Tell me. I want to take my mind off the studio problem."

"I . . . it's . . . it's about you and Kwan. I know it bothers you—it bothers all of us—that there is still so much tension between you."

"Yes, but what can I do? Kwan is unreasonable. I can't work with him. And you know how difficult he made it for me. He never gave me any responsibility, certainly not for anything important. Now that I'm working with Tom, I know what makes a good part-

nership. If only we had more money, I know the expanded studio would be a success."

"I think I know of a way that you could bring in more money **and** family harmony. It won't be all you need to expand, but it could be a start."

"Hana, I don't believe there is anything that can change my mind about Kwan. But tell me what you have in mind. I need a miracle."

"What do you think about giving up the job at the grocery store and going back to work with Kwan part time? Try it for six months. All your classes at the studio are in the late afternoon and evening. You could work at the company in the morning and early afternoon and go to the studio after that. I think Kwan will give you more responsibility. He's very sad and disappointed about how things turned out."

"Sad and disappointed? No way! He's furious! He wasn't even very polite to Tom when he came to the studio. He—" Hyo stopped and looked at Hana. "How do you know how Kwan feels?"

"Mi Sun, Mother-in-Law, and I talked. We all want family harmony, especially your mother. It's too hard on all of us, and family is too important, to let it continue. There must be a way to fix it."

Hyo rubbed his eyes. "I don't want to worry my mother," he said. He sighed, and then he looked a little irritated. "Well, even if you are right about Kwan's feelings, he won't take me back now. And he wouldn't give me any work anyway, so why bother?"

"Kwan took on new projects because he knew you would be here to help. He was looking forward to it. I don't know what happened to change Kwan. Could you try again, for all of us?"

Hyo was silent. *"I'll think about it, Hana. One thing I know is that Kwan will not make the first move. He would lose face."*

"I agree. You will have to ask him."

Hyo sat at his computer the next day during his lunch break, checking his emails. One was from John Baker. Hyo smiled. That was John Baker, the American who sat next to him on the flight from Korea when he came for his father's funeral. They had exchanged emails several times since April. John knew that Hyo and his family had moved to Denver, that he left the engineering firm, and that he was working at the taekwondo studio. But he didn't know why.

Hello Hyo,

Greetings to you and your family from Korea. I'm here on business and thought of you. My meetings wrap up on Thursday, when I'll be heading home. I have a six-hour layover in Denver. Any chance we can get together?

John

Hello John,

Yes, that will work out fine. I'll pick you up and you can come meet my family. Then you can see the taekwondo studio. I have an offer to make to you.

Hyo

Hyo,

Thank you for taking time to pick me up. I enjoyed meeting Hana and your children. Hana is a real artist. Your home and the taekwondo studio are both welcoming and peaceful.

I've thought a lot about your offer to be an investor in the expansion of the taekwondo business. Tom seems like a good man. His vision is clear and his business sense is sound. I'd like to help you out, but with the recent stock market troubles, it's not a good time for me to do that. I'm sorry.

Best wishes to you all. Let's keep in touch.

John

Hyo stared at the email. He had hoped that the plans for the expansion could go forward with John as an investor. Now they were back to the beginning. Would Hana's idea work? Was he brave enough to go to Kwan and ask him? How would Kwan react? He needed to clear his mind.

After his shift at the grocery store, he went to the taekwondo studio and let himself in. He heard voices in the office. It was Hana with a tall American woman wearing a colorful scarf.

"Oh, Hyo. I am not expecting anyone is here now. This is Linda. She is volunteer in my English class. She is artist, too. Linda, this is my husband, Hyo."

"Hello Linda. Nice to meet you."

"Hello Hyo. Nice to meet you, too," said Linda. "I'm helping Hana decide how to decorate the office. She needs a little accent color."

"Please continue. I just came to work out."

The two women turned back to the office.

"This is the painting I told you about yesterday in class. Let's try it on that wall over the couch. It might be just the right colors for this room." said Linda. She held up the canvas over the couch. Hana looked at it from the doorway. The background was a mosaic of bright blues, yellows, reds, greens, and oranges. In the center were light brown ovals loosely clustered together.

"This is perfect, but I cannot buy. Your painting is very expensive for me."

"Don't worry about that now. I'll leave it here on loan. We'll work something out later. In the meantime, you can look for some pillows with the same colors as the background."

"Do you have name for this painting?" asked Hana.

"Yes. I call it Harmony," said Linda.

86

Hyo finished his workout and went into the office. The women were gone. He looked at the painting on the wall. It was calming yet vibrant at the same time. He thought about the questions that were on his mind about Hana's idea. He wanted his brother to respect him. He wanted the engineering company to do well. He wanted to honor his father. He wanted to continue doing taekwondo and be Tom's business partner. He wanted to provide for Hana and the children. But most of all, he wanted to get along with his brother. Discontent was not good in a family. This was not a good model for his children to see and grow up in. He knew he had to fix his relationship with Kwan. He might fail, but nothing would change if he didn't try.

CHAPTER
❖ 10 ❖

The next day, Hyo called Kwan. He asked Kwan to meet him at the taekwondo studio. *"I have something important to ask you,"* Hyo said.

"Can't you ask me over the phone?" asked Kwan.

"I really want to sit down and talk with you," said Hyo.

"Come to my office, then."

Kwan was making this difficult. Hyo closed his eyes and took a silent breath.

"Kwan, please come to the studio. I hope you and I can work out a plan to get along better. Our mother and our wives are both trying very hard to help the family regain some peace."

Kwan sighed. *"Fine. I can be there at six."*

Kwan arrived at the studio promptly. Hyo greeted him. He was glad it was early evening. Both studios were busy with classes. Some students were lifting weights in the weight room, and other students were talking and practicing together. The whole place was filled with activity and purpose.

Hyo took Kwan into the office. Kwan glanced around and stood looking at the painting for a few seconds. Hyo hoped he noticed how nice and organized the office was.

The brothers sat down.

"Kwan," said Hyo, "I am sorry for all the trouble I caused you when I left the engineering firm so suddenly. I left a project unfinished. I know you have been working harder than before to try and make up for my absence."

"Who told you that? Mi Sun?"

"Mother, Mi Sun, and Hana are worried about us. Hana finally asked me to talk to you and make peace, if I can."

Kwan nodded. "I am working hard. But I believe in hard work. I'm not going to let the company fail."

"I know. I want the company to succeed, too."

Kwan snorted. "Really? Leaving was a funny way of showing it."

"I know. I didn't see any other way. But now I think I have an alternative that might help both of us."

Hyo told Kwan that he was willing to work part time. Kwan's reaction surprised Hyo. "I was hoping you would ask for your job back. I need you at the company," he said. "I am willing to take you back."

"Thank you!"

"But I want you to work full time. No leaving at 2:00. I have a lot of work for you. Just come back and everything will be like it was before this taekwondo nonsense."

Hyo's heart sank. He tried not to show that he

was disappointed in this answer. *"I'm sorry, I forgot to offer you a drink,"* he said. *"Would you like some tea or a beer?"*

Kwan smiled. He seemed to think this was the same as a yes to his offer. *"A beer, please."*

Hyo got two beers out of the small office refrigerator. He opened them and the men toasted each other and drank from the bottles.

Then Hyo said, *"You want me to only work with you. You may be worried that my work will suffer or we won't be able to keep up with deadlines. But I want to do both jobs. I can promise you 100 percent effort. Every moment that I am at the engineering firm I'll be working hard on our projects. And I'll train a replacement. I won't leave you stranded again."*

Kwan put down his drink. *"Ah, you haven't changed,"* he said. *"You want everything your way."*

"We both want peace," said Hyo. *"I want to compromise. What's your suggestion for making this work?"*

Hyo saw the look on Kwan's face and knew that this was a good question. Kwan picked up his drink again and took a sip. *"Tell me why you want to work here so badly,"* he said.

Hyo reminded Kwan that, many years ago, he wanted to go to a sports school in Korea. He wanted to compete in the Olympics. Their father wouldn't let him. He wanted Hyo to be a professional, not an athlete.

"This is my chance to live out the dream of my youth," he said.

"That's very poetic," said Kwan, *"But this work is all physical. You're just an exercise instructor here."*

Hyo shook his head. He glanced at his watch. *"Come and watch the beginning of the 7:00 intermediate class. Then let's talk some more."*

Kwan smiled grimly. He put down his drink again. *"Are you trying to convert me?"*

"Yes!"

Kwan and Hyo watched part of the class, and then went back into the office to talk. At first, Kwan still wanted Hyo to come back full time at the engineering firm. He asked Hyo a lot of questions. They ordered take-out for dinner and continued to talk. Slowly, the brothers made a plan. Hyo would work at the engineering firm from 7:30 to 3:00 every day. When there was a big deadline, he would work full time to meet the deadline. After three months, if all was going well, he would start leaving at 2:00.

Then Kwan said, *"Su Jin asked me if she could take taekwondo lessons. I told her no. But now that I've seen the studio and we have talked, I think I'll let her."*

Hyo smiled. *"Su Jin will like it. Dak Ho and Cho Hee come over here after school often. They can all take classes together."*

Before he left, Kwan said, *"This is a trial period.*

I don't know if it will work. I'll try it for family harmony."

"Thank you," said Hyo.

March (four-and-a-half months later)

Hyo parked his car in the parking lot near the front door. At this hour, 7:30 AM, the parking lot was almost empty. The day was cold. It didn't feel like an early spring day. Hyo hurried in the front door. As usual, Kwan was already in his office near the reception desk, with the door open so he could see his employees come in.

Kwan looked at his watch when Hyo walked by. *"Good morning."*

Hyo stopped to talk with his brother. *"Kwan, are you coming to the tournament this weekend? Su Jin is competing."*

"I know. She doesn't talk about anything else. I'm not so pleased about the idea of her fighting, though."

"You can just watch her do the forms," said Hyo. *"But we're very careful. We make sure everyone wears helmets and pads for the sparring. We have strict rules."*

"Maybe I'll come," said Kwan. *"I'm busy with this project, though. It will depend on how far along we are by Friday. How's your project? Are you on schedule?"*

The question irritated Hyo, but he tried not to show it. Kwan was always looking for some reason for Hyo to work full time at the engineering firm.

"Yes. Dan, the new engineer you hired, is a big help."

"Good."

Hyo continued down the hall. Kwan was still difficult to work with. But he gave Hyo more responsibility now. And, to Hyo's surprise, he found the work more interesting. He was learning there was an order and beauty to building roads and bridges. He was too frustrated to notice before.

He understood Kwan better, too. He realized that Kwan had not known how to react to his brother. Kwan and their father worked very well together. They liked the same things. Hyo was different and the change was as hard on Kwan as it was on Hyo.

Still, some days Hyo felt like quitting again. In February, just last month, he met with Kwan to talk about the trial period. Kwan didn't want Hyo to change his hours to 7:30 to 2:00. So Hyo was still working until 3:00. Fortunately, Kwan agreed that Dan was doing a good job. Hyo hoped that soon he could convince Kwan to change his mind about the hours.

When Hyo left the office at 3:00, the sky was grey. The air was chilly. A few flakes of snow began to fall. All evening as he taught taekwondo classes he watched the snow cover the parking lot and the cars. He called Hana during a break to make sure she was not out driving in the snow.

"Were you worried about me?" asked Hana.

"Yes! The snow is getting deep. There must be six inches."

Tom and Hyo decided to close the studio early. The snow was falling hard. By the time Hyo finished cleaning both the front and back windows of his car, the front window was covered again. Slowly, he drove out of the parking lot and onto the street. Usually it took him about ten minutes to get home. Not tonight. The roads were not icy yet, but the snow made it hard to see. He had to stop twice to clean off the ice from the windshield wipers. Finally he arrived at his apartment.

The children were looking out the front window. When Hyo came inside, Dak Ho said, *"Daddy! There's no school tomorrow because of the snow! Mom let us stay up and wait for you!"*

Hyo laughed. *"It's a blizzard."*

Hana came into the room and helped him take off his coat. "Blizzard. *We learned that word today in class. The news said we can expect 12 to 16 inches of snow! The schools are closed for tomorrow. Do you think you'll go to work?"*

The kids waited to hear what their father said.

"I'll decide in the morning."

"I hope you decide not to go!" said Cho Hee. "We want to make snowmen and have a snowball fight with you."

Hana and Hyo laughed. Hana sent the children to bed, and she and Hyo went into the kitchen to have some hot tea. The apartment seemed safe and cozy after the drive from the studio.

"Today is Tuesday, and the news predicts snow all day tomorrow. The taekwondo tournament is Saturday. Do you think we'll have to cancel it because of the snow?" asked Hana.

"I hope not," said Hyo. "The recreation center is booked through August. This Saturday is the only day it's available." He sipped his tea. "But let's not worry about it now. This snow is so beautiful. I think I'll stay home in the morning and play with Dak Ho and Cho Hee."

"They'll be so happy."

In the morning, the snow was still falling. Hyo called Kwan to tell him he wasn't coming in to work. Kwan was not surprised. The snow was so deep that city officials were asking people to stay home except for emergencies, and the highways were closed. Hyo and the children made snowmen, threw snowballs, and walked over to a nearby hill to sled.

95

By noon, the snow stopped and the sun came out. The snow sparkled like tiny diamonds. The only sounds were children laughing and yelling with joy, the "swoosh" of the sleds on the slope, and boots crunching in the deep white powder. Hyo took a deep breath of the cold air. He felt wonderful.

By Thursday afternoon, he was worried. Schools all over the city were closed until the next Monday. Snowplows were clearing the roads, but slowly. Would they be able to have the tournament on Saturday? He called Tom.

"Do you think we'll have to cancel the tournament?"

"I don't know. I've been getting calls from other studio owners all day. They're wondering the same thing," said Tom.

"Would it be better to cancel now and start giving people's money back to them, or should we wait until the last minute?"

Finally, they decided to wait. The forecast was for sunny skies and warmer weather for Friday. Maybe by Saturday people would be able to get to the recreation center for the tournament. Hyo told Hana of the decision.

"That's fine, but I still have a lot of work to do to get everything organized. I have to get to the studio." she said.

"I didn't think of that," said Hyo. He called Tom back.

"I'll come and get Hana in my truck," said Tom. "I think we can make it to the studio."

"That's asking too much of her," said Hyo. "The roads are still slippery and dangerous. The studio will be cold and empty. I think we'll have to cancel the tournament."

Hana put her hand on Hyo's arm. "Hyo, let me help make the decision. I can turn on the heat and all the lights in the studio. I don't mind being alone. Tell Tom I'll do it."

"Really? Are you sure?"

"Yes. You stay home with the kids. I'll go finish the paperwork."

"I'll stay there with her, Hyo," said Tom. "I'll get the equipment ready for the tournament."

Hyo still wasn't sure it was a good idea. But if Hana and Tom thought they could get the work done, maybe he should trust their judgment. He agreed.

After he hung up the phone he turned to Hana.

"Without you, none of this would have happened. You helped Kwan and me get along again. You work so hard at the studio. And now, you're going out when the whole city is closed to get us organized for the tournament."

Hana smiled. "It's not just me. Mother-in-Law advised us. Mi Sun helped by talking to Kwan. You apologized to Kwan and that made it possible for him to ask you to come back to the engineering firm.

97

We all worked together."

Hyo put his arms around Hana. She laid her head on his shoulder.

Saturday morning Hyo, Hana, the children, Tom, and some of the instructors waited at the Recreation Center for competitors to arrive for the tournament. Everything was ready. The floor was taped for the sparring rings and the schedules were ready to be distributed. Tables were set up for registration and the trophies for the winners were on display by a small stage.

Now, where were the competitors? What if people thought the roads were too messy for driving? What if no one came? Hyo and Hana went outside to wait.

At 8:45, the first car pulled into the parking lot. Su Jin, Mi Sun, Kwan, and Mother-in-Law got out.

"Oh no," whispered Hyo to Hana. *"Why are they the first ones here? Maybe no one else will come."*

"Stop worrying so much. Everything will be fine."

Hana greeted Mi Sun, Mother-in-Law, and Kwan. Hyo led them inside.

"Su Jin you go get changed. Kwan, let me show you where you all can sit to get a good view."

"A good view of what?" chuckled Kwan. *"Maybe I'll have to spar with Su Jin."*

98

Hyo laughed nervously. *"We may be a little late getting started,"* he said.

As soon as Kwan and the family were seated, Hyo was needed at the registration table. The referees had arrived. After that, some other studio owners arrived. They shook Hyo's hand and congratulated him on making the tournament happen in spite of the weather. Then, in ones, twos, and threes, people started arriving. Soon, the recreation center was busy. Tom introduced the tournament, and said, "And, here's Hyo Kim, who, with his wife Hana, worked overtime to make this all possible!"

Everyone cheered and clapped for Hyo and Hana. From his place next to Tom, Hyo smiled and bowed. Then, Tom announced the start times of the first sparring matches.

Hyo was so busy for the rest of the tournament that he didn't get to go and sit with Kwan. The day was well organized with almost no problems. Time flew by. Very soon, Hyo was standing on the small stage for the awards ceremony.

Su Jin did well in her forms. She won third place in the sparring. Hyo was proud of his niece. He glanced at Kwan and saw that he was smiling as Su Jin posed for a photograph.

Finally, the tournament was over. The competitors left with their trophies and ribbons. Hyo went and sat down with Kwan.

"Well, what did you think?" Hyo asked Kwan.

Kwan nodded his head slowly. *"When you*

asked me for your job back, you apologized for leaving me so suddenly. I told you to quit this taekwondo nonsense. But, after today, I must say there's more to it than I thought. I'm sorry for calling it nonsense. I can see that you are respected by the students and the other owners and instructors. I can see that you teach your students to respect each other. It's impressive."

All Hyo could say was thank you.

"It's not the same as engineering, but it has its merits," Kwan continued. *"I'm beginning to see why you like it so much."*

Hyo nodded and looked across the room at Hana. She was putting the paperwork into neat piles to be filed.

"People have different dreams for their lives," he said.

"Yes," said Kwan. *"Are you still looking for an investor?"*

Before Hyo could answer, Dak Ho, Cho Hee, and Su Jin came running over. Su Jin handed her trophy to Kwan and grinned.

"Next time, she'll get second, and then first!" said Dak Ho.

Hana, Mi Sun and Mother-in-Law joined the group.

"This is how things should be," said Mother-in-Law. *"Everyone together. Father-in-Law would be pleased."*

Hana smiled. For once, she completely agreed.